THE WIVELISCOMBE STONE TAPE:
LOCAL TALES OF MYSTERY

THE WIVELISCOMBE STONE TAPE: LOCAL TALES OF MYSTERY

*Written and Illustrated
by
Adam Martin*

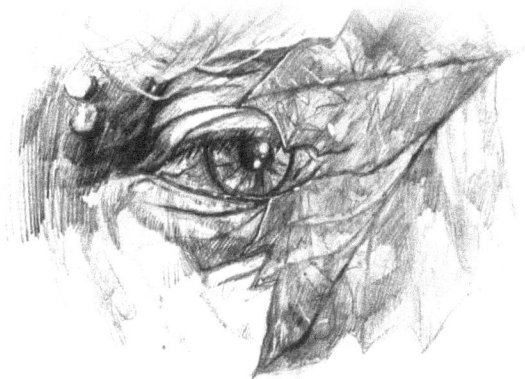

www.adammartinart.uk

Dedicated to all of my family and those who have helped me along the way.

This book is a tribute to the place I will always call home.

Contents

"The Pagan's myths through marble lips are spoken
And ghosts of old beliefs still flit and moan
Round fane and altar, overgrown and broken
O'er tree-grown barrow and grey ring of stone."

Unknown

The Land Remembers:
A Wiveliscombe Timeline

2000 BC – Area is inhabited during the Neolithic period.
500 BC – Iron age hillfort at Castle occupied.
AD 43 - 410 – Roman activity around Castle.
1065 – Edward the Confessor gifts the area to the Bishop of Wells alongside other manors.
1348/49 – The Black Death begins to cause disruption that, along with many other plagues, will continue for years, notably in 1645/46.
1642 – 1649 – Civil War unrest across the country.
1708 – Congregational Church formed.
1807 – Brewery set up by William Hancock.
1829 – St Andrew's Church consecrated.
1911 – Wifela's Combe by F. Hancock is published.
1914 – Slate quarries shut down.
1914 – 1919 – World War I
1939–1945 – World War II
1953 – Secondary school opened.
1996 – Nordens Meadow estate built.
2004 – WHAT (Wiveliscombe Heritage Arts Trail) commemorates the cultural history of the area.
2021- Bishop's Palace remains uncovered in Palace Gardens. [1]

Preface

Many believe that Somerset is a special landscape, one which evokes a sense of nostalgia and longing for those who visit, a potent effect which can become even more pronounced to those, like me, who live there.

Of many kinds of inhabitants, horseback riders in particular will tell that the lands of Exmoor, the Quantocks and the Blackdown Hills emanate a sense of magic and intimidating mystery which is ceaselessly fascinating in the eyes of artists and storytellers. Perhaps it is no coincidence then that the focus of this book, a town called Wiveliscombe, sits comfortably in between each of these regions, acting as a gateway to reputed lands of myth and legend.

The town is already well known for the story of the 'winged/flying cat of Wivey', an occurrence which was documented in an 1899 edition of The Strand magazine, which made the area famous.[2] At the time the feline, called 'Bessie', was considered the next stage in cat evolution, with its 'wings' (which were no more than unusually shaped flaps of skin and fur) allowing it to leap and catch birds. However, zoologists found that it was simply a rare genetic phenomenon. Nevertheless, Wiveliscombe had made an imprint on the world of curiosity, mystery and legend. This story is far from the only tale that the town and the surrounding area has to offer. It is from this landscape that my appreciation for the underlying fabric of folklore that persists through-out the English counties has grown, yet this fabric is frag-ile as much as it is abundant, with many tales carried only through oral tradition and memory.

The roots at the heart of this book go back many gen-erations, yet they have over time become tangled and con-fused. We have over time disassembled the holistic view of the world that once held these stories in higher regard, so it is best to see this book as an act of preservation in the retelling of these tales, adding pieces to the tapestry of doc-umented folklore and supernatural stories across Britain before they are lost.

Tales from the Plague Pit

It was once tradition that in Wiveliscombe on Easter Monday each and every year, at the foot of the clerk's grainy wooden door pinned together by black iron nails, a crowd of villagers would sit together on a swathe of clear open lawn. The ground was emerald and shorter cut than any other patch of the churchyard.

In their gnarled hands, they clutched brown glass bottles of cool ale dripping with condensation whilst wiping their mouths free of the crumbs of the saffron-tinted cakes, clinging to the brushlike hairs of their upper lips. 'This pleasant place is perfect!' – so they thought whilst stroking the luminous grass. Gossip and laughter flowed between them like birds flitting between trees. Soon, the sun-kissed horizon darkened and the children went home, tugged away by their parents.

Once night fell, so the ominous presence of the area had an effect. The air was still and thick, with the hooting of distant owls that swooped silently between branches. Bats cut through the air and flitted away once more into shadows. It became much easier for intimate conversations of ghostly experiences and horrible murders to emerge. Even the clerk joined in and told the tale of the poor old ladies of Bowering's Bottom who failed to turn up for Sunday service – later each found dead inside their cottage, together with blood strewn all over and possessions mysteriously smashed to pieces.

'How horrible…' the mason responded, his long-empty bottle of ale resting on his lap, before clearing his throat authoritatively. He plucked up the courage to tell tales he'd overheard of the ghosts of bed-bound elderly relatives in the village who appeared to their loved ones wearing black cloaks before fading away into the mists of the cleeve, only to be found dead in their sickbeds seconds after the sighting, a cruel omen in the form of a phantom visage.

'So this is how legends disappear…' the clerk sighed, staring intently at the ground below his feet. 'Buried beneath the surface to be condemned, yet from their foundation, our common lives grow in emerald green.' The villagers were slightly puzzled, yet their heads slowly nodded in agreement before they each parted ways. As they left, they each felt like they had taken something away with them. The clerk wasn't far wrong, for few remembered that the bright green grass beneath their gathering spot was left undisturbed for good reason. It was there that victims of the Black Death were dumped into a mass grave and sealed away, never to be disturbed, only whispered of.

Wiveliscombe is not the only town with skeletons beneath its soil. It is important that we all share these yarns, for they are the only threads that seem to be holding together the power of art, history and stories. To be enchanted and inspired is more important now than ever before, however frighteningly true or fantastical the tales may be.

It is documented by F. Hancock that there is indeed a space somewhere in Wiveliscombe that is filled with the remains of plague victims. This is unsurprising considering that the Black Death struck immeasurable damage across the land. It is very hard to locate the specific space today on surface observation, as the landscape has changed; however, we can gather some clues from F. Hancock:

The grass on the ground where they sat [on Easter Monday] had a deeper tinge than the rest of the churchyard…for it was here that the bodies of those who died in the great plague, were huddled hastily and promiscuously into the great pit prepared for them... [3]

In the autumn of this year [1645] the plague broke out in Wiveliscombe and raged through all the next year…Wiveliscombe must have been almost depopulated…Our forefathers avoided, for long years after the plague had ceased, the spot where into one ghastly pit day after day, month after month, the victims of the fearful scourge were thrown. [4]

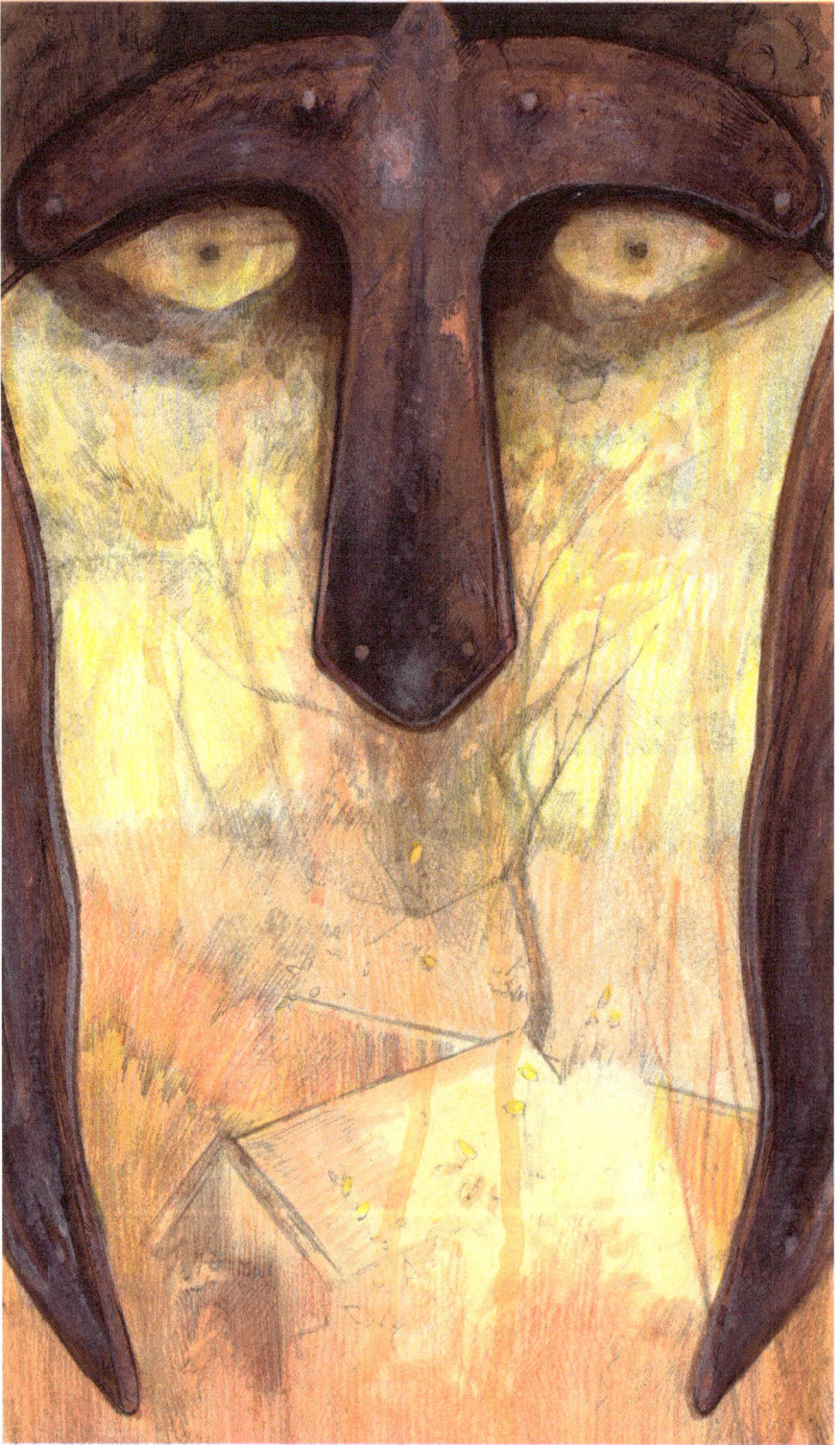

Stone Tape

I used to be ignorant, blind and bound to the apparent linearity of this shell of a life that used to be all I knew. Years and years passed as I grew and developed and I subscribed to this belief without a second thought, but now I see. There are invisible cogs and mechanisms at play that operate beyond a vast curtain which we cannot grasp, in infinite and pervasive blackness, counting by the seconds, hours, years, over and over...

The story began not too long ago with my mother uttering the following words over a half-empty cup of tea on one dim autumn afternoon, as if dictated by an inner compulsion kept hidden inside.

'Years ago, I saw a man upon the embankment...' she remarked, gazing through the window mysteriously. Unremarkable, I immediately thought, yet this could not have been just anyone. The embankment in question is to the south of our home, mere metres away. It is long devoid of habitation and an old railway line used to run along it in the age of steam, until the early 1960s.

When I was little I inadvertently uncovered a long rusted nail from the disintegrated track line, buried in the reddish clay earth in some naive childish attempt to dig up a long-lost relic of a bygone age – a sword or a magic staff

I imagined, but never a nail. Today, however, the embankment lingers, long and overgrown with bramble bushes creating a pocket of shade where overnight frost touches and never seems to melt, sunlight barely encroaching upon the ground beneath its long looming shadow.

Mother continued her sentence: '...he was a Roman centurion. A Roman.' I was confused. How could a figure from an entirely different place in history materialise into the present? I wondered if it could be a trick of the eye or perhaps a lucid dream, yet this would be far more naive than assuming the only other explanation. In broad daylight in such clear and close view, it was just improbable. The light of the sky would have pierced through the gaps between the then-sparsely grown trees and the proud silhouette of such a figure would have been unmistakable.

I racked my brain for an explanation, investigating all that I could, and yet no satisfying results formed. I sat with my laptop and local history texts at hand for hours. My bleary eyes could barely take the piercing glow of the computer screen for too much longer as night after night I searched. My hands began to ache and my gaze stung each time it shifted focus, but soon enough several pieces of evidence began to bleed through – which soon began to describe why this expanse of land could be tied to this Roman apparition, for it was once known as Roman Park. This could not be a coincidence, surely? Amid foggy hysteria, my mind was filled with an ineffable sense that beneath this humble land of the present hides an undercurrent of something else lost and forgotten.

This was what I had been looking for, a spark of something, an excuse to keep looking, and as each layer fell away others followed, a continually shedding and growing serpent. I found that a Roman fort lay less than a mile away; its shell still scars the earth to this day. We lie in a channel that could not have helped but be swept up in the current of the former activity of the Roman settlers. We have since plundered their lands and scraped their remnants, currency and brooches and pottery we find and parade, only after sinking our hands into what was once their earth. Whatever this place calls itself through history, Wife-less-combe, Wyfelescumbe, Wyfel, as much as we proclaim ownership of it and erase the physical remains of our past, we must still be in service to our ancestors.

Once the stone tape plays itself before you, a machination of that which goes on behind the immaterial curtain, it changes you. I have yet to see the Roman, but maybe one day I might. I imagine perhaps on one cold morning filled with vacant thought my eye may snatch a glimpse of the souls who once occupied 'Roman Park', like the flash of a camera or light passing through a stray frame of video tape.

The term 'stone tape' lies in the belief within paranormal fields that some ghosts and hauntings can be attributed to 'impressions' or memories of past events left embedded within the environment. Ghosts that are sometimes referred to as non-intelligent entities cannot be interacted with as they are no more than figments of the past that 'play' themselves before us much like a recording stuck on infinite repeat. It also explains why some spirits are seen to pass through walls or obstacles as such, for they are simply re-enacting the life that they once had, despite the fact that time may have changed and reconfigured the landscape.

Particularly intense emotional events are also meant to form a strong impression of trauma on the landscape that will replay themselves under rare conditions, for example, the cry of a murder victim may replay itself as a disembodied voice years after the event has happened. Therefore, the term 'residual haunting' is sometimes used.

The idea that objects are surrounded by an energy that can be read by gifted individuals in the passing of knowledge and memory is known as psychometry. There has been great debate around the subject. Whilst materials like wood, quartz, and limestone are heralded as ideal substances in storing these 'memories', very little proof has been found. Unlike fossils that are solidified material memories, and problems surrounding the theory arise, as stated by Sharon Hill from the Skeptical Enquirer:

Rocks and building stones can remain for hundreds, even thousands of years, but they do weather and erode. How deep would a figment of memory be encoded into the rock? What happens to the old memories of the rock, such as its origin story often told in psychometry readings? [4]

It has been suggested that defects in the crystal lattice of minerals (the array of atoms that make up a mineral that is shaped by electrical forces) allow for reservoirs of energy. The crystal architecture creates a vortex where memory traces could be stored. These traces could be accessed directly by the human brain later by producing a resonating sound wave or physical pressure such as walking on the ground which we witness as a ghostly occurance.

This specific story is based on a first hand-experience from the 90s, and it is in synchronicity with an old tale documented by F. Hancock, who wrote that:

> At Castle [north east from where the chapter is set] our forefathers believed that on moonlight nights you could still see the shadowy forms of Roman soldiers standing motionless at their posts along the line of fortifications while the moonlight played on their shields and glittering spears. [5]

This raises the realisation that this sighting is not isolated, but adds to what has been documented to have already occurred many times before in the history of the town, increasing its credibility and presenting the fascinating mysteries at the heart of this book.

The Green Men of the
Black Branches

Muggy clouds clung onto the overbearing horizon, threatening a sudden downpour as temperatures climbed. As Aria and her mummy trod up through the meadow, the dry grass scratched at their boots. The reddish earth was solid underfoot, hard and unpleasant to walk over, offering no real grip for their feet to sink into, only dust, dust which floated away on the humid summer breeze.

They held hands as they approached the top of the meadow where they were met by an old crumbling stone wall. The wall was strangled and crushed by tendrils of ivy and roots from several old trees which sat proudly along the top of the hill and atop the wall itself, supported by the earth bank that slanted into the neighbouring field, not ploughed for weeks and humming with crickets and bees. There was an old wooden stile that sat in the gap direct-ing walkers on their journey; the green sign nailed to the wood read 'The Wivey Way', with a prominent yellow arrow directing travellers. Parts of the stile were splintered and rotting, whereas other parts were worn smooth with the oil of the many hands that passed themselves over it on their tracks, assuring the stability of the structure despite first appearances.

'Mummy, help!' Aria waved her arms, hopping up

and down desperately to get help over the stile. She was carefully lifted over to the other side, and then Mummy hopped over herself.

'One day you'll be big enough to get over on your own,' she remarked. Aria shook her head.

'I want to stay this size forever.'

They carried on their journey through an undulating wheat field, gazing ahead at a narrow path carved out through its middle. The wheat wasn't all that tall at this time of year; much of the growth had either been snapped over by the wind or eaten by birds. They passed down the path, watching the black beetles scuttle over the track ahead like heavy traffic through the red dustiness. Aria hopped along before suddenly feeling a slight crunch underfoot – she had stepped upon a beetle but not noticed. She remembered a story she had been told, that when you tread on a black beetle, it causes it to rain…

'I think we should go a different way this time, Aria. How about through the field over there?' Mummy gesticulated straight ahead over the tall bush which stood at the end of the dirt track.

'But…are there cows?' Aria worriedly asked, not wanting to pass through a herd of them.

'If there are, we'll turn back, won't we?' Mummy replied. Aria nodded and Mummy smiled, gazing down at her daughter before leading them into the unknown territory beyond the wall. It was another wide-open field, one wildly overgrown and slanting downwards into a small woodland, surrounded by an uninviting wire fence. None of this attracted either of them.

'I don't like this field, Mummy…there might be

snakes. Or goblins.'

'Oh come on, we won't go that way…look over there, another place we could walk.' She gestured towards another pathway, one which twisted and teemed with sharp brambles at its edges. It seemed to lead somewhere enticing enough to follow, yet it was a twisting path and alive with hostile buzzing and clicking. It was also dark, shadowed by an old fungus-ridden oak at the end of the way, masking what hid around the bend of the track. It was easy to envision strange creatures and monsters that could come crashing from the shrubberies. Once they were on the path, they had to carry on forth to meet whatever greeted them.

There was an old tarnished barn consumed by nature hidden behind the old oak tree, but not much else aside from a field that Mummy had never seen before.

'That looks interesting! I've never been over there before.' Aria tugged on her arm so that they could go back the way they came.

'I don't want to…'

'There are no cows over there, honey! Look! It's empty, I think there's a bunch of wildflowers over there too. Won't you want to see them?' Aria didn't know what she wanted, so she followed along tentatively.

In the centre of the field, they approached a large black oak tree, standing like a remnant from the past, dead yet somehow still alive. Its branches were dense and awkwardly swayed against the breeze, creaking and groaning. Aria gazed worriedly at it until Mummy began to lead her towards it, right beside where the wildflowers were, or so she thought.

'How strange…' Mummy remarked. As they drew

closer the flowers that were apparently visible from afar seemed to fade away, replaced by brush and thistles.

'I wanted to see some flowers. All there is here is this old thing. This silly tree ought to be cut down, it's a bloody eyesore...' She gazed at the crusted sap weeping from the wounds and groaning branches, whilst kicking off pieces of the rotten bark.

'Mummy! Why did you say that?!' Aria gasped, pulling the hood of her bright blue coat tightly over bunched sandy-blonde hair.

'What on earth do you mean?' quizzed her mother with a stern seriousness. 'Oh...I see...I knew letting your father read you those fairy tales before bedtime was a bad idea.' She tugged her daughter's little arm forward, carefully hopping over the stiff spines of dead branches littering the earth below the threshold of the old black oak. 'Then we're going home before it gets too dark.'

'But Mummy...they didn't like you saying that,' Aria cried with a worried wobble in her lips and redness filling her eyes. 'Why won't you say sorry?'

'Because...it's all a load of rubbish! Now come ON!' she demanded, before tripping over a large branch which hooked her foot, making her fly backward into the brambled hedgerow enveloping the field. The thorns clawed at her coat and caught themselves in her hair. She could not thrash around, for with every movement she made, the thorns seemed to dig in further and further.

'Mummy! I told you! Say sorry!' whined the girl, as her mother cried and groaned; the thorns seemed to have trapped her in wiry, evil tendrils.

'For god's sake Aria, get help! I'm stuck!'

'I can't help…the…the green men have got you!' Aria said, with tears falling down her cheeks, staring deep into the cold black branches of the oak tree above. Her mother writhed and pulled as her plastic coat began to tear further and further, white threads of inner lining beginning to fray and strip apart, followed by the idle trickle of blood pouring down her right cheek to her lips where she could taste it. Above them the sky was growing dark and angry, and she regretted traveling this far.

'I knew this wasn't a good idea, we should have stayed at home, why couldn't this have waited until another day? This is ridiculous, I'm too clumsy…although it did seem like some kind of revenge for what I did to that tree. I've heard stories for years about them, that you should be kind to them as Aria says, yet I've always brushed them off as children's stories, laughed at them, but maybe…maybe there is something in it all. Maybe they're spirits, like gods? I pray to God, so maybe I'm just being hypocritical if I don't acknowledge anything else? If gods can exist, why not faeries?'

'The…the book said that you have to be nice to them. The green men…faeries. They're everywhere and if you are mean they don't like it!' Aria shouted, shaking her hooded head, her coat damp with dripping worried tears. 'I didn't want to come here but you did and now you're caught by the green men!'

Her mother paused as she shook in the bramble hedge, as nature began to absorb her. Then after a moment she realised what to say.

'Then…what do they want from me?' Aria paused to think.

'They…sometimes like pasties…and cakes…and

milk. But I don't know what they want.'

'Oh...' Her mother sighed disappointedly, subtly tugging on the bramble binds. It seemed like there was no hope: darkness would come and she would be stuck whilst Aria would probably get lost or hurt trying to find a way to get help. More urgently than that, the brambles were now piercing her skin and bluebottle flies were landing on her nose, examining the area for food. As the tree groaned over her like a wounded deer, crying for her, it ignited a spark within her. 'The tree, the green men...they need help. Look!' mummy said, and Aria looked up and down the trunk. 'The tree is old, it needs love. It's all alone in the middle of this field and it's not very well.'

'Oh no!' Aria cried. 'Don't die, tree!'

'We're...going to help you, OK?' the mother reas-

sured, the brambles around her tight like a rope. The farmland around them was like a waste, uncared for, with the old rotten barn dragged down by ivy and disorganised growths of thistles and dying grass – yet further up her eyes laid sight on something.

'Up there Aria, there's a water tank!' she celebrated.

'Water! Plants love water...'

'Yes! Go and...open it...let the water run down here to the tree,' she ordered, feeling her breath growing shakier by the second, harsh thorns now pressing against her cheeks. Aria nodded and trotted up through the field, waving her arms in her coat towards the grey sun-bleached water tank, gingerly twisting a nozzle which looked like a valve before gallons of water spewed out almost taking her off her tiny feet. The water twisted and turned as it flew down the field, before pooling beneath the threshold of the tree. It drank and drank well from the water soaking into the earth, thirsty, forgotten and mistreated by its carer.

'Hope you like that...' she whispered with a pained smile, the brambles around her loosening themselves tentatively. She dragged herself to her feet and held out her hands, gazing up and down at her tattered coat and the dried bloodstains, looking like she'd been assaulted by some wild creature. She decided quietly that perhaps the best thing to tell anyone would be that she slipped into a bramble bush...not that she was pushed by faeries.

A few weeks later, Aria hopped along a pathway near the black oak tree once again.

'So, Mummy said that she took you this far last time. You're learning to walk further than me!' Aria giggled, holding Daddy's hand tightly, enveloped by the warm green glow of spring and butterflies dancing. The ground was moist after a week of unseasonal rainfall, so they carefully plodded along.

'Daddy, look, that tree!' Aria pointed at the black oak. It had small clumps of green moss growing over old wounds, and bright colourful birds hopping from branch to branch.

'Oh yes, look at that lovely tree. Looks like an oak I think? What a strange place to put it though, must be lonely there in the middle of that field.' He pulled out a well-worn digital camera, which had been in and out of his pocket over the course of the journey. As he walked, he snapped images of everything around him, from interesting plants to picturesque viewpoints. It bleeped as it turned on and the lens hummed as he zoomed the oak into focus. 'What on earth is that?!' He jumped, dropping his camera on a grassy patch beside some daisies.

'Daddy? What happened?'

'Oh…uh…I…I think I just saw…'

'The faeries?' Aria pronounced confidently, with beaming a smile on her face. 'You have to be nice to them.'

'…I think it was, Aria. Yes.' He shook, taking deep breaths as he inspected his camera for damage before smiling in relief. 'I'll tell you what, let's just leave them in peace, shall we?' he asked. Aria very much agreed.

This story is not directly based on any particular tale, but inspired by local faerie legends, as well as spots you can visit around Wiveliscombe which emanate a sense of magic and sometimes danger, evoking a sensation that you are 'being watched'. As well as this, this story is inspired by what we feel sometimes when hiking across the landscape as we may find ourselves in precarious situations caused by forces outside of our control.

There is much faerie lore embedded within the southwest of England, particularly around moor areas such as Dartmoor and Exmoor. Faeries are a much-contested subject, yet there is a documented case around the supposedly enchanted woodland areas of Wiveliscombe, of a man on a walk with his family coming face to face with a 'creature' which seemed a part of the tree he was looking at, camouflaged in much the same way as a moth on the bark of a tree. Apparently, as he moved closer to the face, it gave him a startled look and then disappeared – yet he was not afraid of what he saw, rather, he was filled with a great sense of joy at having seen such a creature for himself.

Once you go and explore in areas such as the woodland of Wiveliscombe, the moors of Exmoor and supposedly enchanted places such as Wistman's Wood on Dartmoor, it is easy to feel the sense of 'magic' and wonder that is evoked from our deeper instincts. Nature itself is so full of fascinating things that can be seen as magical in many differing aspects.

It was rational in the eyes of our ancestors that such things could only be the result of supernatural entities, who inhabited enchanted 'pockets' we could visit in our own reality. Some also believed in parallel realms accessible through portals. The visitation of these pockets or portals could result in encounters with fairy folk. [7]

Faeries are one of the most varied and contested topics of note in folklore, with associations to all manner of other interconnecting mythologies and belief systems, even that of the legend of King Arthur. One consistent point, however, is the necessity to stay on their 'good side'. As in certain known faerie sites, one must supposedly treat them and the land with respect or face their vengeance. [8]

The damage they can inflict upon humans who find themselves unwelcome or disrespectful guests is not limited to simply pinching and pushing, but even extends to paralysis. In the home, faeries can attack us, enacting punishments for being lazy or poor housekeepers. They may choose to hide things we need from us, such as car keys, or make us trip up by tying the laces between two shoes together. Perhaps in this sense, their existence is there to remind us all to look after ourselves and our planet as a whole. [9]

Blackened Hills

Would have left sooner,
Before the clouds turned black,
A hollow sky before me,
Up Maundown on horseback,

Contain my wretched fears,
Masking my anxiety,
Ignore the cruelty of years,
To withhold my own piety,

Let pain flow down the stream,
And leave my muses in the trees,
To discount the wooden beam,
The gibbeted fool sees,

Do not think of him,
Now, can he see me?
In light flickering so dim,
No, he watches thee,

Steed quivers like a leaf,
Shoes clatter upon stony tread,
Ground vibrating beneath,
Where he was left for dead,

In an iron cage, rotting, lost,
His cries carried for miles,
Flesh bit by aching frost,
As bodies fester in piles,

A black veil falls,
We press on up the hill,
I turn my head from the calls,
From his cries bones chill,

Me and my steed,
Our own business we pursue,
For the dead, there is little need,
To lead our fortunes askew,

So I paid him no thought,
Yet my horse was not content,
To leave without wrought
And leave his purpose exempt,

And the black veil falls,
In panic and further dismay,
My steed, whining, calls,
In horror I cannot convey,

Maundown Hill was alive,
As the trees would hiss,
I pray only to survive,
The revenant's wretched kiss,

The gibbeted man had come,
Although I couldn't see,
Our fears were the pure sum,
Of the horror in front of me,

Me and my steed of white,
Did charge far away,
In our hearts deepest fright,
To return only in light of day

There is something in that earth,
Buried should it stay,
Touched by a darkest curse,
For it will always be this way.

The story of the ghost of Maundown Hill, towards the west of Wiveliscombe, was found in a passage from Wife-la's Combe: A History of the Parish of Wiveliscombe by F. Hancock, who notes the spot on Maundown Hill where a man was hanged in chains for matricide and his body left grinning at passers-by on horseback. Once the body had disappeared, however, his apparition was still witnessed and was said to spook travellers and their steeds as they headed about their business at night around Maundown Hill. [10]

It is true that a man was left there to repay his horrific actions, yet it is mysterious to hear the manner by which his memory lingers, supposedly haunting travellers. It is true that even today the entire area has some essence of eeriness to it, perhaps stemming from the quiet breeze or the creeping sense of desolation.

Blackened Byways

A thin winding pathway,
Walls high on one side,
Trees that leer over the sideway,
Where souls shook and cried,

A path carved by time,
Mud thick and dark ink,
Unraveling a dirty crime,
In earth blood would sink,

The lone blade came along,
In the moonlight glint,
His wife, children, everyone,
Did scrape bone, like flint,

Another byway blackened,
By the cruel hand of man,
Yet time cannot lacken,
What fading memories can.

II

A long winding byway
Trees high on each side,
Shadowing an ancient pathway,
Where underfoot he lied,

Carved by clattering carriages,
Layers forced further down,
The vibration of passages,
Through the passing of each crown,

A poor soul lingers,
Hidden under his remains,
Under crossroads poke icy fingers,
Bound his spirit in chains,

Out of hope, he was driven
The little that such life gave
His body lies hidden
Under path, an unmarked grave,

Not a madman nor crook
Left here in shame,
For his own life he took,
No one takes blame,

Another byway blackened,
By the poor nature of man,
Yet time cannot lacken,
What fading memories can.

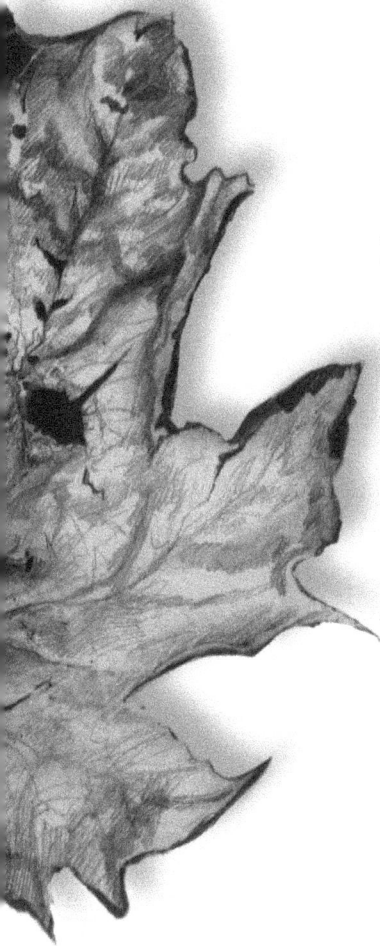

A popular story from the parish is that of 'Cutthroat Alley', a small lane which heads towards the neighbouring fields from Style Road between two houses. It has been told that a man murdered his family here (his wife and two children) with a silver blade. However, as is always so with word-of-mouth tales, details can become foggy and other accounts say that a murderer escaped down this lane to mop the blood from his blade with a rag. Whatever the truth may be, the lane itself has earned a worrisome association with murder and foul human cruelty; today it still carries a sense of this along its long and old stone wall, which once carried on along its full length — until a newly built housing estate was established, removing a sizeable portion of it entirely around 2016. The majority of it still remains today.

The second part of 'Blackened Byways' is a well-known story in the area, that of Jews Lane and a victim of suicide named Tytibye, said to be buried somewhere beneath its tracks at the crossing leading down to Greenway Lane. Because he committed suicide it would have been uncustomary to have him buried on consecrated ground at the time, thus he was buried beneath the footway with a stake driven through him.

There are two significant points to raise about this piece of history, related to our ties to ancient customs and beliefs. Firstly, there is the idea that individuals who led harsh lives or died with 'unfinished business' could rise again as revenants, vengeful spirits or even vampires, due to limited understanding of how the human body decayed. If there was suspicion that someone may have been a vampire or revenant, the body would be exhumed. From there, the naturally decomposing body would show bloody lips, nails and hair that were still growing, and pale skin – which were often mistakenly seen as signs that a person was coming back to life during the night. If it was decided that this was occurring, a stake would have been driven through the chest pinning them to their graves. (In places such as eastern Europe, many bodies were buried with bricks in their mouths to prevent vampiric fangs from emerging.) Secondly, the positioning of Tytibye's grave at the crossing of pathways is also significant, as there was once an ancient custom where suicide victims were buried at crossways as a method of spiritual protection for the nearby village.

The lore of this story ties into both long-held beliefs and the contemporary emergence of what some have seen as an apparition of the spirit of Tytibye, standing over the place where he is buried, perhaps proving him to be such a restless spirit. This is said to be the spiritual fate of many victims of suicide across the world, a good example of which can be seen in Aokigahara, or the Japanese 'Sea of Trees', which has become better known worldwide as the 'Suicide Forest'. This is an area of dense woodland over thirty kilometres wide to the north-west of Mount Fuji, and an international hotspot for thousands of recorded suicides, said to be haunted by countless 'Yūrei' (ghosts of the dead in Japanese mythology) who are tied to the earthly plane. The forest is supposedly incredibly quiet, ominous and isolated, a description which can be applied to the crossroads at Jews Lane too. Whilst it is a public footpath, who knows how many travellers are aware of the story which lies right beneath their feet.

C. 1970s local map of field names, sourced from S-M, Farrington (2005) *Wiveliscombe*.

Ford

Pitt Farm

Lower Grant's Farm

Ford House   Weir

LANDS

MIDDLE MEAD

SLOCOMBE PIT

MOOR AND LOWER MEAD

G.P

Castle Farm   KILN CLOSE

THE MOOR

TWO ACRES

THE FOUR acres

Castle Quarry (Disused)

MIDDLE TOP Field Camp

FIVE ACRES   FOUR   THREE ACRES

EASTERN

BARN CLOSE

CLAY STOPPERS

LOWER MEAD

SOUTH TOP Field Castle

Hyden Wood

EASTERN PIECES

PLAIN CLOSE

R.F. NEWTONS

S.P

SECOND WORDENS

Lodge HYDEN WOOD

BOTTOM FIELD

FOURTH BEERS ASH   Manor Farm

Castle Bridge   BOWSLADE   GREAT BOWSLADE

FLOORS

MEADOW

Wiveliscombe M.S

SEVEN ACRE FLOORS

TWELVE FLOORS   EASTER

CHEEKS COX'S MOOR

EIGHT ACRES

TWELVE ACRES

AUBERRY MEADOW

SWEETHAMS

GREAT AND LITTLE MEAD

ALLOTMENT

DRY FIELD

TWELVE ACRE FIELD

Furzymoor Barn

SIX ACRE MEADOW   LOWER MOOR

FATHER MEAD

Earthwork

5 ACRE FIELD   MOOR

EIGHT ACRE MOOR

MIDDLE CLOSE

GREAT FURNICAPS

LITTLE

FURZE MOOR   GREAT MOOR

Washer's Farm

FRY'S THREE ACRES   Fry's Farm

Fire and Sandstone

The devil is evil incarnate, a trickster and a liar. His aim is to corrupt the soul of man, God's image, through manipulation and temptation. The devil may succeed occasionally in tempting some of us from our holy paths but he has not, and cannot, control the greatest force of creation, nature itself. One cannot reason with a hurricane, and here the devil is powerless – yet there was an occasion in 1827 when his ego overstepped possibility.

The sandstone tower of Saint Andrew's Church had developed a threatening crack. It groaned and crumbled as if it was about to tumble down. This in itself was evil's doing, as the devil had planned. He had manipulated the masons to make silly errors in their work, yet it did not go the way he envisioned. As he watched carefully from between the black iron bars surrounding the churchyard, disguising himself under a grey cloak, he cursed and shook his fists in frustration, the crack was meant to send the entire tower tumbling down, yet it did not! He stroked his chin, pondering the next move in order to bring about the tower's fall.

'If I cannot manipulate man to trash that cursed tower...,' he hissed under his breath, '...then I shall use nature!' He shuffled away on his cloven hooves, disappearing into a cloud of black smoke.

Soon after, the devil returned with a plan, to seek a force of nature: a dragon. One had been lying in wait for centuries for its call to be heard hidden ina field near the Church, and the devil could hear it groaning above the trickle of streams and hissing trees.

The devil reappeared at the edge of a stream that ran copper red. The church tower loomed in the distance, taunting the devil. 'I am tired of hiding!' he squealed, excitedly peering into the redness below him, until a creature began to emerge, stretching the length of the channel which cut right through the entirety of the field. A salamander of suffering. Its head was like an arrow, and its eyes lay flat on top brimming with mystery. Its skin was a great copper stain upon the rich emerald of the grass around him. It seemed pleased to be awoken from its slumber, until the dreadful devil looped a chain around its neck. He cackled, clutching the iron chain-links proudly in his bony fingers. The dragon burned the land upon where it stood until its wings unfurled like sprouting leaves after winter. It set off into the sky under the will of the devil who rode it proudly like a steed.

A black shadow crept upon the land, reaching the churchyard, and the devil launched a torrent of hellish boulders upon the tortured tower. The attack was relentless, shaking the foundations of the town itself, the dragon's wings beating as the devil held on to the beast with the iron chain around its neck. He cackled and wailed, and the salamander dug its talons deep into the brickwork, roaring with the force of a crashing tidal wave.

The air was thick and hot like syrup, stinking of hellish sulphur. The clouds were grey and gathered above, rumbling with the crash of thunder, until the sky opened up with specks of rain, pricking like needles upon the devil's back. The first few drops evaporated before they even touched the skin of the accursed creature, until the atmosphere turned to a chill. A downpour unleashed itself, and the dragon's cracked sandstone skin revealed itself to be no more than dried mud which began to run in the deluge, revealing jade gems for scales and intricate markings like that of a serpent. The devil roared in anguish, tilting his accursed horns skyward in anger, and the beast shook its wings in revolt.It was clear now that they were at odds with each other, locked in their own battle of wills. The turn of the weather had more than changed the atmosphere, it had changed fate.

The air cooled and the land below the church became a damp mirror in the driving rain. Looking at his reflection, the devil knew he had to escape, but did not know how. The beast he had tamed was not his own, but of mother nature. His knuckles were bony and white trying to hold on to the writhing muscle of the salamander.

The thunderous rumbles subsided as through the clouds broke golden sunshine. The beams of light were a beacon of hope for the entrapped dragon, who flew towards them to safety, shaking the chain around his neck away ferociously, sending the devil tumbling to the damp earth below with a cry and a splash. The salamander escaped the grasp of the devil and shot away into the hills, flying west until his green scales dissolved into the fields of emerald surrounding the town.

St Andrew's Church in Wiveliscombe was where the devil himself was said to have arrived astride a huge emerald dragon, hurling stones upon the newly built church tower, only to be vanquished by St Andrew in dramatic fashion. The dragon symbol is the cipher of an eternally renewing force of evil, harassing each generation in an ageless form. Essentially it is a force of corruption upon the souls of the innocent, only to be slain by a hero, such as that of St George, patron saint of England. The tale of George and the Dragon, therefore, is a coded message conveying the slaying of corruption and sin by Christianity. It is more than just good versus evil – it is a story of eternal renewal of evil and corruption and the ceaseless persistence of those with the hope and ability to fight against such threats.

With the abundance of dragons in modern culture, the mainstream fluidity of such a symbol can lead to confusion over its true meaning. Many see the dragon as a polyvalent symbol, one which ebbs and flows with each period of history. Its presence is felt in every major mythological system across history, and with each mythology, it is imbued with a different meaning. In the medieval mindscape of England, the dragon was seen as an ever-present evil to be destroyed by good. However, the idea that the true seed of the monster comes from our primeval encounters with predator reptiles, resulting in a combined beast built up in our ancestors' minds as a residual memory for our species today, seems most likely. The seed of this truth has spread to birth countless dragon beliefs, as attempts to make sense of our world – and even our universe itself.

Babylonian mythology has the body of the great dragon Tiamat as what brought forth the cosmos, with her body after death birthing the universe. Tiamat is the chaos and darkness whose destruction at the hands of bright spirit Marduk brought about order to our galaxy. At the same time, in the world of alchemy, the Egyptian dragon Ouroboros (or 'tail eater') is the symbol of unity and infinity in the quest for the philosopher's stone, the seed for gold. The dragon image for alchemists was a cipher, a way of guarding their elusive secrets and experimental developments. Different images of dragons would symbolise different materials and processes – for instance, raw material would be a green dragon, a winged dragon was for a volatile element, and the opposite for a stable element.

It's curious to see how such an aspect of myth has been used in our quest for scientific discovery and understanding of our world, and this goes much further. Some time ago, mountains, earthquakes and volcanoes were seen as the bony spine and troubled dreams of a slumbering dragon. Often dragons beneath the land were explanations for such features – and, in truth, this was not far from fact, if we consider the turbulent magma and shifting of the earth's mantle which forever keeps earth at the mercy of mother nature. Features of the landscape such as Worm's Head in Rhossili are obvious catalysts for myths and legends of such beasts. One could argue that perhaps, if there was no such fascination with dragons as a part of our mythical mindscape, then we may have not made the same steps to understand and appreciate the true nature of earth's powerful processes.

I See a Darkness

It was her first morning working as a maid to the family of farmers, the Waldrons of Maundown Top, a broad hill that helped shield Wiveliscombe from the cascading elements. Winter opened up with its cold harsh embrace for the young girl.

Whilst she was awake and ready for work, the family were still tucked up, wrapped in each other's arms. She envied them, the parents Jonathon and Beatrice with their children Ivor and Sage in the bedroom opposite, whilst she was outside the farmhouse alone and shivering but eager to start work. She reminded herself of her duties, that she had made a good and early start so that she might form a good impression of her work ethic. For a poor girl like her, no other argument could be made. Her own family was a mystery to her, and she had none of her own brothers, sisters or parents to care for, so she knew that she must adopt the Waldrons as if they were her own.

'Money…for sharing my…love…and care to them… that's all it is…' she whispered under her icy breath, teeth chattering and nose dripping as the breeze cut through her. It wasn't long before she recognised a problem: the darkness of winter made it nearly impossible to see anything clearly, through a freezing cover of mist that caused strands of spiderwebs draped over shrubs and bushes to look like glass. Thus, she searched for a match for her candle, one of the few things she carried along with her inside her modest sack of possessions.

Without disturbing her custodians, she headed back inside and pulled each drawer in the kitchen out carefully, eager not to arouse any suspicion of snooping, as much as to avoid making a loud noise. She crept around the corners of the dwelling and jumped as the family sheepdog groaned when she shuffled past, laid with his jaw resting on the cold cobbled-stone floor. His weary eyes looked up at her before slowly closing shut once more. She was lucky that he didn't cause a fuss, yet somehow to the maid it felt like he knew what she was doing and so did not wish to disturb her.

'Good boy,' she whispered, smiling at him, yet her search dragged on uselessly. The building was still so unfamiliar that the matches could have been anywhere in the dim light. The chances of making a good and early start on work seemed to be delayed until sunrise, until…something caught her eye. There was a light beckoning from the other side of the field, with a soft glow accentuated by the mistiness. As she headed towards the door to see, it became clear from whence the light was emerging. She could just about form an image through the mis: the light's source was within what looked like an old dilapidated farmhouse, one much the same as the current residence. This one, however, she had heard about before. Some speculated that it was haunted and had no owner, with walls stained in blood. Yet, somehow, something about the building still appealed to her with nostalgic charm.

From the kitchen table, she took up her unlit wax

candle and stepped outside once again, gently pulling the door closed. Diligently, she trod towards the shattered ruin, a place that seemed to absorb the darkness from all around it. She knew that she was being brave, and that from desperate times, it was necessary to enact upon pure needs in order to survive.

The marshy earth sucked her feet deep, letting cold wetness irritate her toes. She struggled in the absence of light, staggering across the field and towards the warm beckoning glow which bloomed in the softness of the icy morning mists. The brittle black structure grew ever nearer; as she glanced back at the Waldrons' house, all that was once visible was now shrouded in encompassing mist.

When she got to the ramshackle building, it was obvious that no other option remained but to face fear, uncertainty and temptation to step inside the dark building, and find out the origin of the strange source of light.

Gingerly she set herself within the threshold of the building, gently tapping on the flaking warped door. After some wait, it creaked open slowly and out of the gap peered a pale old man with a pointed, wiry grey beard.

'Ah...hello my dear,' he greeted through a toothless grin.

'Hello...I...I'm sorry to disturb you, but I do not have a light, could I borrow yours?' She raised the candlestick towards the man, offering it whilst shaking with cold and nervousness.

'Oh...yes...yes, yes I can help with that.' He gestured her inside with a thin bony arm. He was covered in a black velvet robe that seemed even darker than the surrounding shadows. It was a reluctant offer to accept, yet he insisted on leading her inside out of the cold, into a hollow and dusty dwelling with wallpaper peeling at every angle and spiders milling in and out of the gaping cracks and holes.

He led her into another room, from whence the fiery glow spilled. It was a room panelled with wood, and the air was thick with dust which tickled her throat. Therein sat two more old men at a circular table, each taking turns scrawling on a large parchment with a scratchy black quill, unaware of her entrance and completely absorbed in their own activities. Between the two of them sat four candles, lit and dancing with every measured breath they took.

Carefully she reached over and with a piece of straw laid on the table, ignited a tentative flame on her candle. She backed away thanking them quickly, unsure of the three strange inhabitants, eager to get back to the Waldrons' before daylight, before they realised she had gone. The man with the toothless grin had a knowing, beady stare which followed her as she shifted backward – until her feet caught the threshold of the door on the way out, sending her stumbling.

'God preserve me!' she whined and suddenly the candles extinguished. The room fell into blackness. Then the old men vanished along with their parchments and gowns. Breathlessness clenched her throat and her bones seemed to freeze in place, as she lay stunned on her back in the middle of the strange house. Her flame was still alight but it was weak, seemingly confirming that the experience was real – yet all other remnants of the scene had gone. The house was lifeless, aside from her.

Before the flame could disappear, she lit the candle again in her shaking grasp and at that instant, bellowing flames shot up the chimney and the entirety of the wood-panelled room becoming a blazing inferno, one which was cold and harmless. It was unnatural – she felt no pain nor heat, and quickly assumed she had entered some form of afterlife somehow.

Perhaps I died when I hit the ground? She pondered and her trembling body cowered as the room was enveloped in a nightmarish blaze which seemed alive as any natural entity – the lapping of the waves at the shore or frost crawling up a bedroom window, shining in the winter light.

The living flames slowly recoiled from the walls and windowsill, leaving no trace of damage, gathering in the centre in a pillar of fire above the maid, who gazed at it in pure disbelief and terror. It assumed the shape of a figure, a giant, that loomed over her judging her every fibre carefully, as tall as the tip of a church spire and as intimidating, a pure embodiment of whatever heaven or hell may exist beyond the life of flesh and blood. It had no face or distinguishable features that she could make out. Soon it toppled and fell onto its feet, cradling itself and crying a shrill whine like that of an owl, bursting into a scattering of embers which pricked the maid's skin.

There were no words to describe her encounter, no manner by which anyone could ever describe such an event and be believed. Whether it was an omen of good or bad was unknowable until the smouldering pile of ash on the floor cleared itself, revealing a small envelope. It was sealed with wax and clearly old, perhaps older than even she, an envelope that was clearly there for her to see, and her only. With shaking fingertips and icy breath, she picked it up off the ground and opened it without a second thought. The

writing was hard to decipher in flickering candlelight, yet it was soon clear what she held in her hands, a blessing which could not be rightly questioned. The house deeds were finally found and her name was scrawled within them, by an apparent distant relative whom she never knew but somehow knew her.

Finally, after years of decay and neglect, the building had found its rightful owner, as was always meant to be.

This tale is extracted from a mention in F. Hancock's Wifela's Combe of 'The Legend of Maundown Top'. It is incredibly hard to trace any kind of origin behind the tale, and it may well be a story which has been passed down from generation to generation in the town – warning of a place it would be unwise to set foot within, tied to stories of murder and bad fortune, and connected with other ghost stories in the area and others like it.

Fields of Bones

2 December 2019
Local Journalism

*D*o large felines still roam Exmoor? That has been a question asked time and time again over countless years by the residents of Wiveliscombe and beyond, as numerous sightings have been recorded in and around the area – but as yet it has been one left unanswered. Recently we heard from local student Adam James Martin, who gave us two compelling first-hand tales of his own sightings around the area that he hopes do not cause too much worry for livestock keepers and residents.

'I recall several years ago, around 2008, a sight witnessed on the fringe of Exmoor near Wiveliscombe. I was on a school trip exploring the moorland until one way or another I found myself alone, close enough to local habitation to not feel lost yet far enough away to feel some sense of isolation. What I saw was nothing that many would obsess themselves over, for it was merely the carcass of a sheep left in a deep ditch at the edge of open moorland. However, it had not simply died of natural causes, for its body was torn to shreds with little but bones and wool left scattered about. Leaves were entwined with the curls of wool and through tiny holes in the bones small insects crawled through. It is entirely possible that this is no more than another freak instance of loss of livestock, for the sheep could have easily fallen victim to the bitter wind and freezing cold that so often falls upon the lands here, its body pecked and bitten away at by foxes and crows, a feast of flesh. Even domesticated dogs can claim the lives of such creatures if their vicious nature becomes unleashed. With that said, however, something about the carcass was unusual in the way that had been seemingly hidden in the ditch away from obvious view, stowed away for a later meal. Not to mention the bones stripped clean with undamaged ribs, the red stains of where muscle used to cling still visible. This image lingers in my mind to this day as something unusual. The way those bones jutted out from beneath the wool, holding it up like a rotten canopy. I recall how Exmoor once played host to wild predators like wolves; surely it must be simple enough today for a small community of large predators to be sustained across the UK?'

'I also roughly remember a day several years ago, around 2006, when I saw what I consider to be a big cat when glancing down a pathway carved out by farm vehicles as we travelled towards Wellington – seeing the rear of a large black beast swaying its tail from side to side, walking away from us. We'd travelled too far to turn back and see what it was for sure but I wish we had, for then we'd know a bit more of what to make of the stories.'

These stories only add to the curiosity surrounding the Beast of Exmoor around Wiveliscombe, yet many people will mock the possibility that the story has any substance. Those who do should have a meeting with local resident, retired huntsman and former marine sniper John Matthew, who kindly invited us into his home to discuss his incredibly compelling encounter with the beast of Exmoor around thirty years after his involvement with 'Operation Beastie', a military effort to capture the beast after a slew of mysterious and savage cattle deaths around Exmoor. We didn't have a set of specific questions to ask John; we only asked that he shed us some light on his involvement in 'Operation Beastie' to offer a fascinating insight. Perhaps his testimony would suggest that maybe this story isn't as far-fetched as many would first believe? What follows is a transcript taken from John as he spoke to us from his home in Wiveliscombe.

'I was with the Royal Marines for a while until I left them just after Operation Beastie, and you know, it's the one regret I have through my entire career that still gets to me. I guess becoming a hunter afterwards was kind of my way to get back at the mistakes that were made during this operation [gesturing at stuffed animal heads on the wall of his living room]...at the time, the media loved the Beast of Exmoor tale, they ate it up, any story that came along they blew out of proportion, so when I was asked to take part in an actual hunt for the 'thing' I was sceptical. Lots of people said that the creature was a supernatural monster or something like that *but I knew that, if it was something real, it could only be a large animal, so I painted a target in my head and stuck with the idea of catching it once and for all. When I got to Exmoor to hunt the thing, I was taken to the fields of dead cattle first to examine the 'crime scenes' they jokingly called it, but they were no joke. There were sheep with their throats ripped out, blood everywhere, carcasses torn at and bitten by something unlike anything I knew of living on the moors, certainly no fox or dog. I knew then that something here was very strange. I didn't know what, but I wanted to take my time with it, allow some moments to examine the scenes, do a bit of detective work to actually try and track the thing down...Before I had a real chance to though, we were hurried along into our ghillie suits [worn by marines as camouflage, featuring simulated pieces of turf to appear as one with the landscape] to put on a fanfare for the media circus. I was festooned with face paint and twigs so that my face was obscured from the media who had cameras everywhere, although I got off lightly compared to others...I don't think it was worth it all. I mean why would we be wasting time and energy entertaining them when we should be out there in the field? On the whole, it was frustrating for us and the farmers. They were worried that we were going to be driven out by the media attention and not be able to kill the thing taking their livestock. I just don't think that the papers ever considered that they were disrupting a strict military operation...it was ridiculous.'*

What we were doing wasn't a laughing stock in my eyes, nor to the farmers whose livelihoods were being disrupted by all this. Some of my troop weren't taking it seriously so I gave them a stern talking-to, said that if we were the ones to ac-

tually catch this beast, then we'd be famous the world over, maybe write a book or two, grab a Hollywood film deal! That surely tempted them…but still Operation Beastie felt like a game of make-believe even when we were surrounded by murdered ewes. That was, until we found ourselves on Exmoor in pitch darkness…as soon as the lights went out things got serious, it was just like any other warzone. The snipers we used were equipped with SLRs with image intensifiers with lethal effectiveness to a person up to 2,500 metres, which on open moorland seemed like the perfect set-up, if not for a few things that added complication to our operations like [sighs] the media once again who kept on breaching the perimeters we'd set up. Sometimes we couldn't tell if it was a sheep's arse or a photographer bent over in a field! They were persistent, didn't give two hoots about shuffling through cowpats and brambles to get an 'exclusive' on the beast…but they weren't helping anybody, hell they were probably spooking away the sheep. The police eventually tightened things up a bit so that we'd have the darkness to ourselves to actually concentrate on our jobs, which was much appreciated, but still we would reach daylight to find more dead sheep, this thing slipping through our nets again and again. It makes me mad…I'm sorry, I feel like we had a golden opportunity with this operation that was wasted.'

'We'd pop off in the morning for some breakfast in a nearby B&B – I think I was living on egg and toast for about three days at this point. Each time we'd all sit together and have the same conversation.
'Seen it yet John?'
'No…not yet.'

They'd always snigger at me, making jokes and imitating my words in a stupid childlike voice to make me sound simple. 'What? Tonight might be the lucky night,' I'd always add just to try and keep morale high, even if it was crumbling. I think one of the innkeepers heard me, whilst I was sat in her poky wooden breakfast chair wiping crumbs of toast off my mouth. She shuffled over to me and told me to close my eyes and hold out my hand, then in it she placed this chain with a tiger's-eye stone dangling from the bottom polished to a narrow point, like a tooth I thought. This had to be a good omen if I ever experienced one. She even winked at me as she walked away wishing us good luck. I could taste the jealousy in the air from around that table pouring from my comrades, they didn't tease me at all after that morning.'

'Eventually it was obvious that this operation had outstayed its welcome. All involved were getting more and more edgy and frustrated and the farmers wanted the thing dead, for all they could see was more and more sheep found torn apart with all but their bones left behind – 'like fish at a restaurant' I remember one saying, and I must add that I found it very hard to disagree with that. There were scores of orphaned lambs being locked in temporary shelters, being bottle-fed each morning…the cries that they made were heartbreaking every time I heard them. They sounded pained and lost like they knew what had happened to their parents, but in some strange way they encouraged me even more to catch this damn creature. Of course, we couldn't make any mention of big cats to the press, it was strictly to be referred to as a 'rabid dog' or something…nevertheless, it was nearly a week on and still we had caught nothing. Then Friday night came…I was *perched near a farmhouse on the edge of Exmoor watching through my night sight. It all seemed oddly quiet that evening, no foolhardy journalists or wayward sheep, just a bleak and hazy view from my sniper's perch. I put on that necklace I was given in some vain attempt to cough up some luck, but at this point I decided that anything that would help the cause was worth a try.'*

I then spotted something, a dark mass of movement near the farm. My heart started racing...it was huge, some kind of animal surely, not a dog or horse, something much more... feline. I had my finger glued to the trigger, trying to pace my breathing along with my heartbeat so that my sniper scope did not wobble too much as I just watched this creature stroll near the farm. It was clearly a big cat, it had to be. I was watching the Beast of Exmoor, but I couldn't fire a single shot at it! He was too close to the farmhouse, directly in my line of fire – it was like it knew that and so chose to use it as cover. I couldn't risk the shot, so I just watched it stroll away, out of view and out of my sniper's effective range, the most heart-wrenching frustrating moment of my entire life playing right before me...it was only then that the word 'cat' started being tossed around, but to the papers I still had to maintain the 'dog' stance, a large rogue dog. That was it, to me the whole endeavour was over...Once the papers deemed our efforts inadequate they set a bounty on the beast, dead or alive, which killed any chance that we had stone cold. It was hard enough trying to avoid civilian casualties, but now we had the prospect of amateur hunters stumbling about in the dark with their stupid sawed-off shotguns, either shooting innocent livestock or one another just for some prize money!

It was all completely irresponsible. We had no choice but to pull out and call off Operation Beastie…and so the slaughter continued, and we had to leave behind more fields of bones.'

'I will never live this down; I became a hunter afterwards for a while just to try and reclaim some pride after I had a chance to nail that beast, but I am not redeemed. I know that here in Wiveliscombe there have been sightings of more beasts, especially in the outer reaches towards Bampton, the Blackdown Hills and so on…I'll take another shot at it if I can, that's what I live for now.'

It certainly has sparked interest and perhaps forces us to question: do we really know what is and isn't possible within the natural world? And how do you track down what may not even exist?

This story is largely made up of real testimony from eyewitnesses. The incident referred to in the beginning involving the Army is based on an event which happened on Exmoor in 1983, where the Royal Marines were sent to investigate for weeks after a large number of cattle were found slaughtered, all showing signs of a big cat attack. Although the investigation yielded no exact proof of existence, it has not ruled out many explanations, which range from escaped zoo animals to pets that may have been released into the wild and survived. Mysterious big cats seen outside of their natural habitats are known by the code 'ABCs' (Alien Big Cats), and have been seen all over the world, even as far as China.

Paranormal creatures of the wilderness, such as the Beast of Exmoor, Black Dogs, ghosts and so on, are considered to stem from a practical function established in early human traditions: as a method to prevent children from wandering afar onto the moors and into the wilderness. The idea then was to make the landscape seem as lonely and terrifying as possible, inhabited only by scary and dangerous mythical creatures – which may have become what we know today as the Beast of Exmoor. There are a multitude of noted contemporary encounters in and around Wiveliscombe.

I saw what was probably the Exmoor beast between Wiveliscombe and Bampton early this morning…looked more like a large wolf than a big cat…
(J. Petts, 19 March 2010)

A big cat or several cat-like animals live on Exmoor. This cannot be doubted, I have seen them.
(J. Foster, 12 December 2008)

I have been instructed never to go into the forests alone without a rifle or a hunting knife and in the company of an alsatian! Having lived in London for forty years I had been fed the lie that no such beasts existed in the UK.
(L. Napier-Burrows, 16 July 2012)

[11]

'Driving from Wiveliscombe towards Clatworthy early one morning this summer [of 2016], an experienced game-keeper and stalker saw a big black cat in a field. "It was the size of a Labrador,"…There is speculation

that this animal has moved territory from Waterrow.
There have been numerous sightings of a big, black
cat in that part of the 10 Parishes, but none in recent
weeks, since an area of ground where it is thought to
have slept had been cleared of scrub. Claw marks have
been found there, high up in a tree...'

[12]

In principle, this story is more naturally based than
supernatural. Pumas and panthers are capable of adapting
to our landscape with many sources of food available to
them such as livestock, deer, rabbits and foxes. Big cats are
even known to live in the cities of warmer climates unno-
ticed by the general population.

To many, the presence of big cats in our countryside
is a large problem for us to contend with from an
ecological point of view, as they pose a threat to local
wildlife. The fact that they are still being seen may indicate a
breeding population, and the moors and forests of England
are a lucrative hunting ground.

The chance we have of crossing their paths is slim,
but may not be impossible as contemporary stories tell us.

The Screaming Cold Embers

I listen to what he remembers,
Calling to him from the white cold embers,
Screaming to him in the dead of night,
Calling moans from when once bright,
Wailing howls from where she lay,
Choking on her steaming ash she'd pray,
With creeping burn swarming pale skin,
Burning and scolding eternally within,
She still calls out from itching pain,
And her draping locks disappear again,
In that fireplace where her vessel lay,
Her voice is still heard again today.

Foxes whine from bleakest black,
And calling owls swoop their track,
A living soundtrack to night-time ventures,
In death, she calls from the screaming cold embers.

The source of this tale is a primary case heard from an old school-friend. At the time, he lived in a cottage opposite St Andrew's Church which I passed on my way to school each day. On some occasions, I would come inside to meet him and sit down for a while beside a large, obviously very old (possibly Victorian), brick fireplace which dominated the living space. According to the source, that fireplace is apparently known to be where a maid or housewife fell and burned to death. Furthermore, it is apparently where the sound of a female screaming has been heard in the dead of night, which would align with the story itself. No other evidence has been found or heard since; however, the concept of an isolated traumatic event seemingly 'replaying' itself could again be linked with the stone tape theory.

The Grey Traveler

The tale of the grey traveller is short, but that does not diminish its mystery. In fact, it is its brief nature that only amplifies its curiosity. The details I am about to unfold are all that are known of this case, for it has been decades since he was first seen at Wiveliscombe station on the twenty-fifth of April, 1938.

Grey as the plume of steam from the engine he disembarked from, the traveller arrived in the town. His appearance was unusual, for his face was covered by a mask and a broad-brimmed hat shrouding his already minimal profile in shadow. He had a look of unfriendliness and hostility, not wishing to allow anyone the privilege of seeing his true self.

Along with him there was a lady with flowing raven locks of hair and bright lips of cherry colour, clad in a black fur coat. She seemed to be unlike the traveller in every way, and begrudgingly carted a mountain of luggage behind her.

Together, they pressed on. They trudged around the corner from the church, past the terraced houses and up the cobbled incline into town. The poor lady dragged their mysteriously immense pile of luggage behind whilst the traveller headed forth. Not a word was ever said between them.

The couple disappeared into a guesthouse on Town Hill, and the next morning, they vanished, never seen again, leaving no trace of their arrival, but only whispered stories. They simply disappeared silently and strangely into the same plume of smoke that they arrived in.

Perhaps they were spies, or escaping conflict from one part of the world to another, using Wiveliscombe as an escape route?

The remains of a station in Wiveliscombe still exist, but the track is long gone. The mystery may never be solved.

The Strike of Twelve

It was said that some decades ago in the parish of Wivel-iscombe there were two particularly distasteful inhabitants, a pair of nasty old men who shared a rotten, crumbling manor house far away from anyone else in the community, shrouded on either side by a small woodland, within which they only ever frequented a small selection of rooms.

They were both retired and forever promised to restore the estate to former glory, but time forever seemed to escape them. Thus, it remained a place where they could writhe and meditate upon their own immorality and scepticism, not so far away from civilisation that they had to traverse far as they staggered home from an evening's merriment at one of the many local drinking establishments. They chose to stay far away from the town so as not to be consistently disgusted by the droves of people who marched into church, particularly on a Sunday, nor caught up in the jovialities of local people who lived out their happy and perfect lives, not to mention the loud schoolchildren who giggled and screamed as they chased each other home every day. They saw them all as 'marching sheep bleating with the rest of their flock' who often made joy in mocking them, singing terrible vulgar songs and laughing in the face of their traditions. The naive would find their songs confusing whereas everyone else found them disgusting.

Every Friday, at around five o'clock, they were there without fail to begin their crawl and at each place they set foot in they were met with disgust from the folk sat inside, yet they gave no cares for the jeering and mumbling insults. They sat minding their own business, sending verbal rebuttals very rarely, and when they did they were venomous and putrid, often consisting of no more than a few choice words, mentioning wrinkly wives or ugly children – in short, more than enough to earn them a fair number of bruises.

Even though they looked upon all with a wrinkled nose, they still knew everything about each little person and their family, especially after overhearing so much gossip. Arguably it was hard to avoid such tales with the loudness of voice with which some people spoke, especially after a few drinks. Yet the miserable pair, as much as they despised the people, still loved this gossip, and they took it along with them as they left every evening, whether they left with or without injury. The odd scuff on the eyebrow or split lip was a small victory to them, a badge of pride for how rotten they could be to others, a strange achievement of which to be proud. This routine of theirs went on for years and years…until old age started to tear them down. Visits to the local pubs became less frequent and fresh news of the village folk became thin on the ground until eventually, it was completely non-existent to them. There was a distance between them and those of the outside world.

Years later it was said that one of the old fellows became bed-bound with sickness and they had no visitors, for no one truly cared for them. The bleakness of autumn and winter became sometimes truly unbearable on their frail hearts and they began to ponder the afterlife from the cold bedside.

'What if…there is a heaven…or a hell?' one of them pondered in the bleak evenings, as the rain pattered against the smeared cobweb-ridden windows.

'Nonsense, it's the human condition. Existential terror. We cannot handle the infinity of nothingness.'

'But…what about all these ghost stories?'

'Stop it, now. The brain sees what it wants to see. We are no more than atoms and cells. That's it.'

'But…what if?'

'Listen…if there is an afterlife, you come and visit me at the strike of twelve midnight after you pass. Tell me all about it, understand?' He fearfully agreed to shake his hand with his cold, frail fingers – for he knew that if there was such an existence, then there would only ever be one direction that they would be headed. It was neither north, south, east or west…but downward.

Not long after the contract between them was formed, the time came. The survivor tossed about sleepless in his bed, unaware that his friend had passed on at the other end of the corridor on the strike of eleven, merely thirty minutes after they had set themselves to sleep. It was deafeningly quiet in and around the house. The rainfall that had bombarded the leaves on the trees had ceased and slowly trickled away, and so too had the wind faded into absence. It was as if the whole world had gone away, leaving a night hollow and empty, setting the stage for the terrible revelation as the clock struck twelve, sending a mechanical chime down the hallway from a withered old grandfather clock, disrupting the once-eerie peace.

At the foot of the survivor's bed a bright yellow flame burst into existence on the twelfth strike, and from its dreadful cold aura emerged the astral presence of his friend, eyes hollow, sunken and white and his skin barely clinging to his brittle bones.

'No…I don't believe it!' the survivor cried, shrouding his face from the unearthly glow of his astral friend. The ghost reminded him of the deal they had made, with a voice that shook the crumbling walls. 'What…what did you see? Oh, tell me…please!' The words tumbled from his lips and his bones shook in rigid fear and disbelief, as he faced the frightful truth. The ghost spoke with a pointed finger.

'Mark me…' he said, growing nearer to his friend with an angry, terrified stare. 'There is a God, and a just God. Yet…there so too is a Devil, and a terrible one! If you don't mend your ways, you'll be where I am now! Look here…' He reached into the wooden panel at the end of the bed, burning five holes into it with his burning white fingers before he withdrew his hand then disappeared into a cloud of white ash forever. The survivor lay still, terrified and rigid, peeping over the quilt to the five holes left behind.

From there, he prayed and prayed for what felt like days, confessing himself to God, laying bare his sins for all and any who might listen, begging for forgiveness for the miserable life he'd led, for all the people he had upset and the joyous events tainted by his filthiness. Slowly but surely his joints locked themselves into place, freezing solid, until his fearful rigidness became eternal. The house fell silent, he at one end of the corridor, his friend at the other. Maybe it wasn't too late to change his ways – none will ever know, for in death, they were destined to face the greatest punishment, to be eternally alone.

Though large, fast-paced cities may well have their own ghost stories, there is something about towns such as Wiveliscombe where history and folklore live and breathe more naturally alongside each other. The story here is one which has been documented by F. Hancock, who notes it as a 'popular ghost story' in the town's history, yet offers no explanation of who these men were, where they lived or indeed how the events may have come to unfold. [13]

Entities

You may wonder what it is about humanity that makes it so reliant upon stories, fantasy and escapism. Is the bare face of meaningless existence so hard to deal with? Or the fact that after we pass on there is…nothing? It is the last great frontier, something that we cannot measure, less well documented than the ocean floor or the blackness of space, an unknowable cosmic antithesis to our busy everyday lives which seem to always take vital importance…yet we always come back to stories as a divergence from the here and now. Why is that?

History is absorbed and recorded in our stories; the legend of King Arthur has been shaped by the passage of time, by each hand that has touched him, injected and polluted by the views of the hand that feeds his tale, as have countless others over time. It is a cycle of growth, one which blinds us to the truth of what once was. History and legend go hand in hand, but sometimes they are not always their own individual entities. History and legend can become one and the same, cyclical and infinite, a serpent eating its own tail – creating a form that in Wiveliscombe may have once been called a wraith or a banshee, but which we today call a ghost.

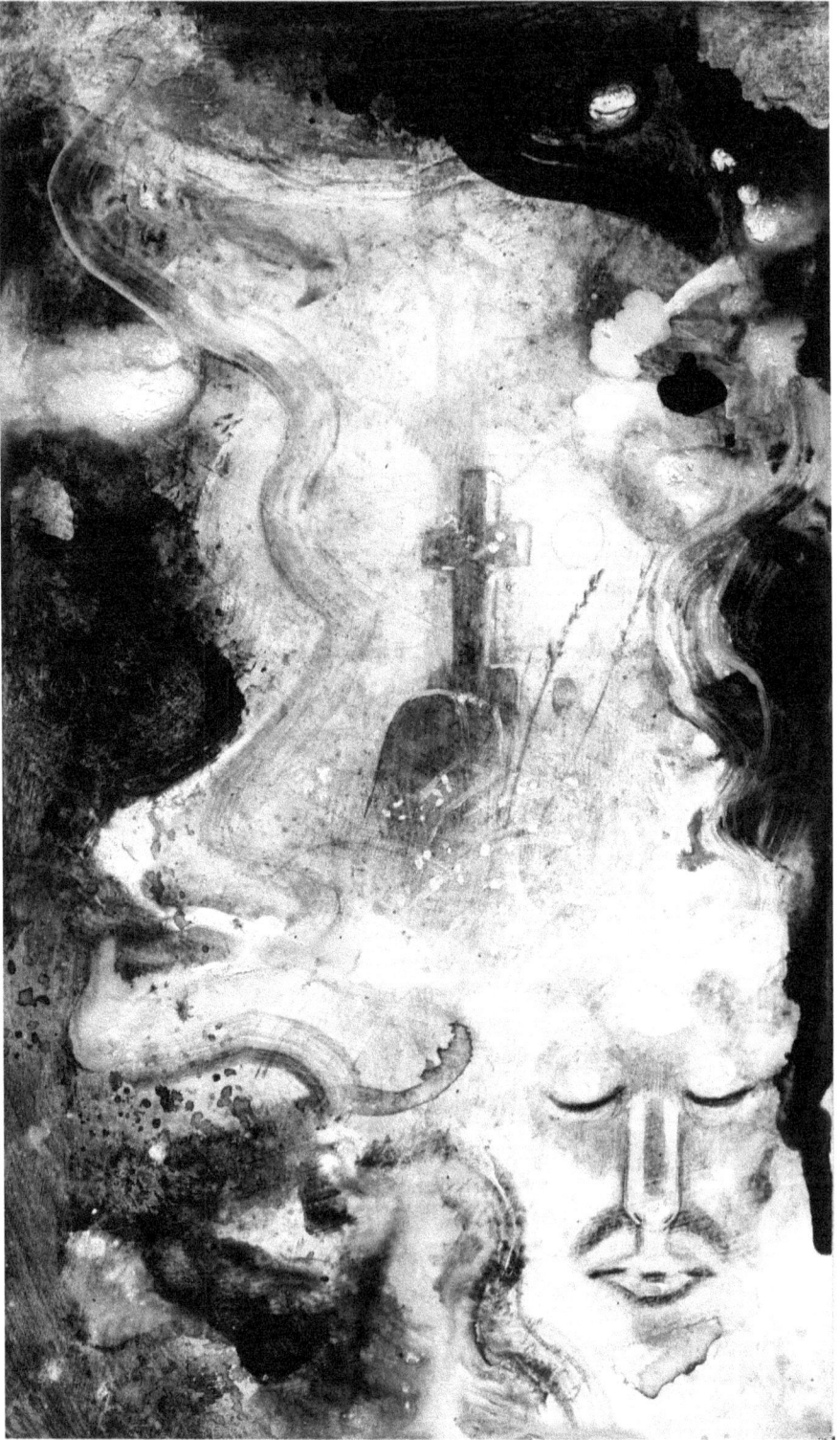

I

In the summer of 2004, I saw a tall black shape, almost like a rippling robe yet simultaneously unlike any fabric. It contorted like a thick dark haze, rising in broad daylight from the foot of some old stone stairs, that lead up onto ground level from below the graves of St Andrew's Church from the adjacent gravel pathway. The speed at which it disappeared from view was unnatural; it darted into the alleyway beside, through an old wooden gate with a flaking and rusted handle. In the bright summertime light, this entity was the exact opposite. It pervaded the soft green leaves and softly blowing grass sprinkled with white and yellow flower heads, unmissable and immediately apparent, even far away.

It has not been seen since, yet is far from the only time it, or others, have been witnessed, for some claim to have seen 'black rippling shapes' in Wiveliscombe for decades. It is a persistent entity that still exists even in the eyes of children with no knowledge of its history or reputation as a wraith of local repute.

There are even some stories that refer to black rippling shapes in churchyards as 'church grim', the souls of the most recently interred who are now bound to be protect the consecrated ground from evil – that is, right up until the next person is to be laid to rest. The wretched burden then is passed onto them, picking up where the last soul left off.

II

In the very same grounds, two more souls have been experienced, of which little is known aside from the incidents that led to their discovery.

Sometime in November 2013 the first unveiled itself. At around eight o'clock, within the cold wintery walls of the church, having just been delving into the crypt to help shift crates of second-hand novels out of the mould and damp, I compulsively decided to sit in an old wheelchair made of wood that was lingering dusty and motionless near some old tombs. It was cold and slippery from the dank moisture that hung in the air, so I quickly left it alone before venturing up into the church once again to aid a friend in the task at hand.

We stepped inside the church again, so peaceful and quiet with not another soul in sight, and crossed to the southern half. Large tapestries of woven gold thread hung proudly, and crackled old oil paintings framed themselves against deeply set, perfectly whitewashed walls with undulating archways. We exchanged chatter, before we paused our conversation…we could never have known what was to follow. In the void of silence that was left, a raspy cackle emanated from nothingness in front of us. Someone was standing there, paralysing us each in fear for what felt like an eternity, blood rushing to our heads and a tense ringing sounding in our ears.

What followed shock was the primeval instinct to

run, to escape the unseen and the unimaginable. Whatever created such an unearthly sound was surely some kind of evil; perhaps I had connected with something through contact with the old decrepit wheelchair in the dank old crypt below? I can never tell. It is far from the only creature whose shrill cold laughter has been heard, however.

III

It was around six o'clock in October 2011 as I walked with my mother. Nothing was visible around us, only the cold orange lamplights that flickered with the wings of moths, giving us guidance along with the empty glow from the windows of a nearby row of cottages on Rotton Row.

We chatted all the way down until we reached the wall dividing us from the churchyard. It was too tall to see over, but we knew that with the darkness there would be nothing to see there anyhow, as tempting as it always is to peek over the tops of built-up brick walls to see what they hide. It was peaceful and it was silent…until that too was broken, this time by the isolated and disembodied hollow giggle of a young girl that seemed to burst over the stone wall as if someone was standing just behind it – yet that 'someone' did not exist (in the physical sense at least). We looked at one another and sped up our steps towards safety as fast as we were able to, far away from that place. We still wonder what, or who, we heard to this day.

IV

Further into the bustling town I have heard of a particular soul with a taste for mischief, affectionately known by many as 'the baker', a poltergeist. He has been known to cause disruption, knocking over books, throwing objects whilst employees quietly try and work in the shell of his former bakery sitting near the top of the hill in town. Each business has had the same keys passed over to them with blissful ignorance of its unimpressed lodger still clinging to his work. Down below in the basement, it has a heavy and intrusive feel, like trespassing when nobody is home – at least, no one that we can see.

V

On Grant's Lane, there is a stone upon which moss may never grow, for it is consistently prodded and marked by locals as the site of a notorious murder in 1856. The area continues to spark fear and uneasiness to this day, with disembodied sounds and shadows, especially as the sun goes down.

VI

At Castle, a full moon may appear to glint from the spear of a lost Roman soldier, still patrolling his home as if it were still standing before us today, like time has frozen on an unwound pocket watch, cyclical and ever repeating the same moment. It forces one to realise that the only thing we have in our lives is memory, that even the present is a fleeting moment, which is gone as soon as it is noticed. Despite this, these soldiers still march onward, and they have been seen on countless occasions.

VII

Then there is the recreation ground which sets the stage for an urban legend, a murmur through brittle and broken branches. The question is this: what could possibly be odd about the sight of a young girl in a pretty white skirt playing on a set of swings at the park? The answer is simple – if it happened to be late in the night and beckoning upon the witching hour. Suddenly the once sweet and joyous image is inverted into something altogether more sinister. The distance at which her pale silhouette has been seen rocking back and forth on rusty chains make her woes unfortunately unclear.

We do not know whether she may be bitten with sadness or merely adrift and at peace, or a stray frame from the stone tape. Her skin and dress some say are apparently pale enough to be luminous in the blackness of the late

night, and her face too vague to distinguish. She has been witnessed very scarcely, so maybe she is merely a figment of the imagination. At least that's more comfortable to believe in.

Ghost stories surround us; they come uninvited in black and white, they come with sticks and stones and they come with cries and groans. They are here, the only kind of story that has no ending or explanation. Once you become a part of one yourself, you'll understand why.

F. Hancock's Wifela's Combe refers to many entities seen in Wiveliscombe, specifically to *strange creatures seen curling away in wreaths of black smoke* [14] which is a fairly common paranormal encounter seen by many experts and investigators across all areas of the world. It is also said that Wiveliscombe residents have for a long time shared a belief in banshee spirits.

Each of the ghosts mentioned in this section of the book are drawn from contemporary paranormal experiences. Part of the compulsion used to drive forth the creation of this book was the urge to create a collective of the major and lesser-known and unheard legends that have embedded themselves within Wiveliscombe.

A Wiveliscombe Field Guide

There are some characters in the tapestry of Wiveliscombe legends that are notable for their curiosity, for multiple reasons...

Witches

It is a mistake to say that witches do not exist in the contemporary world, as they undeniably do. All manner of magic is still being practised in a wide kaleidoscope of cultural landscapes.

There have been stories around Wiveliscombe of strange encounters with witches for years. One account documented by F. Hancock from around 1900 tells of a hunting party being sent scattered around a woodland in terror after coming across what is described as; *Old women on broomsticks with wraiths and goblins.* [15]

Whilst each of us has a different understanding of how magic can be defined, the 'witch' term has been used as a shameful excuse to persecute and murder innocents for centuries. It was once believed that anyone accused firstly of being a witch and secondly of 'cursing' someone would then have to be cut 'above the breath' to draw blood, which was believed to break the curse.

In 1823 a lady called Anne Burges was severely lacerated on the arm after being accused of witchcraft in Wiveliscombe; her attackers were fortunately found guilty and sentenced to prison for four months in Taunton Gaol for the attack. [16]

Banshees/Bean-sí

In Irish folklore, the cry of a banshee is seen as a dark omen of someone about to pass away in a family. There are similar superstitions surrounding owls, whose calls are sometimes heard as omens too.

According to Katharine Briggs, the banshee term simply means 'fairy woman', so has a multitude of meanings and possible origins. [17] The belief in this powerful omen was once very respected in Wiveliscombe, perhaps seen as a useful sign by some, but nevertheless one which filled most people with dread.

It is possible to say that the fairly remote location of Wiveliscombe, at the gateway to Exmoor and surrounded by rolling hills, perhaps meant the power of nature itself generated such beliefs, as it is easy for the imagination to become enchanted by the power of landscape, especially at night. Hooting owls, crying foxes and other creatures can each sound fairly otherworldly and inexplicable when heard in the pitch-black, when one may decide to wander about in the landscape of Wiveliscombe after dark.

Squire Yea &
Hellhounds

Hellhounds are a common folklore belief across England. They are on the whole depicted as large black dogs with flaming red eyes, which stalk the moors and hills of rural areas of England. They are well documented all over the country, and inspired Arthur Conan Doyle to write 'The Hound of the Baskervilles.'

What is interesting in Wiveliscombe is that the story has been combined with a mysterious figure called 'Squire Yea'; it is hard to say what exactly this connection meant, but there is a strange reference in the parish register of Wiveliscombe from 1725 which states: *In 1725 was buried John Steevens, who was killed in Mr. Yea's quarry.* [18]

'Mr. Yea' may be referring to a member of the Yea family who had close associations with Wiveliscombe through properties such as Okehampton House.

This story seems to be a variation of the tale of Squire Cabell, a Dartmoor ghost story. There are multiple versions of his story, but it seems that to some, Cabell has become a leader of the Wild Hunt, a ghostly pack of hunters who bring misfortune to any who may stumble across them, riding across the moors with their baying hellhounds. Richard Cabell, like Mr Yea, was a real figure who in death has gained folklore association with both the Wild Hunt and the canine supernatural force of the hellhound.

Sightings of the Wild Hunt were first recorded in 1127 in the Peterborough version of the Anglo-Saxon Chronicle.

They were described as a huge and ugly party of huntsmen riding upon goats and accompanied by horrifyingly dark black hounds. Observing the Wild Hunt, as with sightings of hellhounds, was almost invariably an omen of misfortune.

This story likely stems from the historical context of the period, where child mortality was at a high and only two out of three children managed to live to the age of five:

> ...it's easy to imagine, as the autumn nights begin to draw in...how the eerie cries of the unseen creatures rightly signal the mortality of vulnerable old folk and children which a sharp northern winter would inevitably bring. [19]

In 1712 Wiveliscombe had been struck with a terrible smallpox outbreak which resulted in no less than 117 burials:

> The terrible disease seems to have carried off, like the plague in earlier years, whole families...There seem to have been funerals every day during this afflicted year [of 1712]. 1721 was also a very unhealthy year...[then in 1725 Steevens perished]. [20]

The time of Mr Steevens's death, along with the emergence of the tale of Mr Yea and the hellhounds as a supernatural force in Wiveliscombe, seems to further indicate that stories of hellhounds and the Wild Hunt act as a coping method drawn from the despair created by difficult periods of high mortality... or perhaps Mr Yea still roams the countryside in the guise of a modern day huntsman along with his fearful loyal hounds, tracking down their next victim.

The Green Man

When visiting Wiveliscombe, you may see that there are three totems which stand on a raised area of earth visible from the road which leads to and from Taunton and Glastonbury. Upon these totems, a Green Man is visible at the very top of the left totem, whilst other Wiveliscombe icons make up the others, like blocks of cultural heritage stacked upon one another.

The Green Man symbol is actually a rather new development compared to other Wiveliscombe supernatural creatures such as hellhounds – and unlike other creatures in the pages of this book, the Green Man symbol stood proudly at the gateway to Wiveliscombe is in fact a sign of resistance.

He is a force which has roots in mythology, drawing comparisons with the Green Knight of Arthurian myth and the forest-dwelling Wild Man. However, he has been revitalised in the contemporary world to represent the preservation of nature against industrialisation. Stories are a part of this, as storytelling it is a unique facet to human nature that no other creature on earth can benefit from.

The Green Man is the perfect representation of what we should aspire to be and perhaps who we once were as a species, in harmony with nature. Without stories, without a natural world to coexist with and share, and without respect for nature itself, we have no future to look forward to.

Magic Spaces
Views of Wiveliscombe that
helped inspire this book.

PLATE I- *Brewery view near 'Cut-throat Alley'.*

PLATE II- *Bleak winter fields.*

PLATE III- *St Andrew's Churchyard.*

PLATE IV- *Fields behind Nordens Meadow between seasons.*

PLATE V- *Old trees leading to the grave of Tytibye, Jews Lane.*

PLATE VI- *Church view.*

PLATE VII- *Steps carved into the old railway embankment, where a Roman soldier appariton was spotted.*

Appendix

Mythology

Mythology, folklore and legends are stories which are timeless and exist outside of reality, although they are inspired by real concepts or events. They become exaggerated and twisted, but sometimes they sit fairly close to physical reality. In this way they differ from reports of paranormal phenomena, where supernatural events are genuinely claimed to have been witnessed or experienced in person.

The difficulty we have today with accepting myths is that we are generally taught not to have a holistic view of the world. Perennial philosophy, on the other hand, is a perspective which suggests that everything we experience in our lives has a divine superior parallel that is eternal and far richer than what we can experience on earth. This means that myths are the closest contact we have to this outer realm. *The myths gave explicit shape and form to a reality that people sensed intuitively.* [21]

Before organised religion, gods with distinctive identities did not formally exist. The most ordinary elements of the world, such as the weather or the harvest, were divine because they had a divine meaning, and our own world was just a shadow of that truth. The system of mythology is essentially a kind of compass to explain the conundrums of human life that we still grapple with today. Why do we exist? What is our purpose? What lies after our time on earth? They are an art form that allow us to transcend our physical reality through ecstasy, so that we may attempt to touch this 'divine' realm that we intuitively feel the existence of. No other living being on earth aside from humans asks these questions about existence – which may present the impression that we are, as humans, at the centre stage, closer than any other living being to transcendence:

If professional religious leaders cannot instruct us in mythical lore, our artists and creative writers can perhaps step into this priestly role and bring fresh insight to our lost and damaged world. [22]

Wiveliscombe Geology

The town is sited on sandstones of Lower Permian age (290 million years old)....

These rocks are not uniform and a good contrast can be seen by comparing the exposed finer sandstone in Sandy Lane [pictured opposite] *with the pebbly sandstone in the cutting on Grant's Lane...*

Wiveliscombe enjoys a widespread reputation for good fertility with the land suitable for both arable farming and grazing.

The landscape is characterised by gently rolling hills, small covets and patches of woodland, some deeply sunken trackways and long sinuous enclosure hedges dating largely from the early 19th century. [23]

Sandy Lane, with its characteristic sandstone composition that Wiveliscombe is known for. Perhaps the geology of the area plays a factor in the stone tape theory as explored from page 20.

End Notes

1 - S.-M. Farrington, *Wiveliscombe: A History of a Somerset Market Town* (Wiveliscombe: Colden Publications, 2005).

2 - Farrington, Wiveliscombe, p. 268.

3 - F. Hancock, *Wifela's Combe: A History of the Parish of Wiveliscombe* (Wiveliscombe: Barnicott and Pearce, 1911), p. 245.

4 - Hancock, *Wifela's Combe*, pp. 196, 197.

5 - S. Hill, 'Spooky Rocks', *Skeptical Inquirer 27.3* (29 January 2018). <https://skepticalinquirer.org/newsletter/spooky-rocks/> accessed 7 April 2019.

6 - Hancock, *Wifela's Combe*, p. 253.

7 - J. Kruse, *British Fairies* (Street, Somerset: Green Magic Publishing, 2017), p. 30.

8 - D. Mullis, *West Country Faerie: How and When to See Nature Spirits* (Cornwall: Bossiney Books, 2010), p. 38.

9 - Kruse, *British Fairies,* pp. 106–7.

10 - Hancock, *Wifela's Combe*, pp. 251–2.

11 - 'The Exmoor Beast: Fact or Fiction?' Toad Hall Cottages. <https://www.toadhallcottages.co.uk/blog/exmoor-beast/> accessed 2 December 2019.

12 - L. Sloan, *Wiveliscombe Messenger.* October 2016.

13/14/15 - Hancock, *Wifela's Combe*, p. 248.

16 - Farrington, *Wiveliscombe*, p. 275.

17 - K. Briggs, *A Dictionary of Fairies: Hobgoblins, Brownies, Bogies, and Other Supernatural Creatures* (Middlesex: Penguin Books, 1977), p. 16.

18 - Hancock, *Wifela's Combe*, p. 199

19 - C. Larrington, *The Land of the Green Man: A Journey through the Supernatural Landscapes of the British Isles* (London: I.B. Tauris, 2015), pp. 98, 104.

20 - Hancock, *Wifela's Combe*, p. 199.

21 - K. Armstrong, *A Short History of Myth* (Edinburgh: Canongate Books, 2005), p. 5.

22 - Armstrong, *A Short History of Myth*, pp. 4–11, p. 155

23 - Farrington, *Wiveliscombe*, pp. 2–5.

Bibliography

C. Larrington, *The Land of the Green Man: A Journey through the Supernatural Landscapes of the British Isles* (London: I.B. Tauris, 2015)

D. Mullis, *West Country Faerie: How and When to See Nature Spirits* (Cornwall: Bossiney Books, 2010)

F. Hancock, *Wifela's Combe: A History of the Parish of Wiveliscombe* (Wiveliscombe: Barnicott and Pearce, 1911)

J. Kruse, *British Fairies* (Street, Somerset: Green Magic Publishing, 2017)

K. Armstrong, *A Short History of Myth* (Edinburgh: Canongate Books, 2005)

K. Briggs, *A Dictionary of Fairies: Hobgoblins, Brownies, Bogies, and Other Supernatural Creatures* (Middlesex: Penguin Books, 1977)

L. Sloan, *Wiveliscombe Messenger.* October 2016.

S. Hill, 'Spooky Rocks', Skeptical Inquirer 27.3 (29 January 2018). <https://skepticalinquirer.org/newsletter/spooky-rocks/> accessed 7 April 2019.

S.-M. Farrington, *Wiveliscombe: A History of a Somerset Market Town* (Wiveliscombe: Colden Publications, 2005).

'The Exmoor Beast: Fact or Fiction?' Toad Hall Cottages. <https://www.toadhallcottages.co.uk/blog/exmoor-beast/> accessed 2 December 2019.

Author Biography

Adam Martin was raised in Wiveliscombe, gaining a passion for art and writing from his inspiring teachers at Wiveliscombe Primary School and Kingsmead School. Since then he has earned a first-class MA from Plymouth College of Art and a BA(Hons) from the University of Plymouth. Alongside producing prize-winning artwork for the BBC and FOX TV, he has persued themes of mythology and folklore, producing a self-published novel in 2017 exploring Arthurian legends.

He has been drawing inspiration and knowledge from his home town to develop this book, coagulating history with retellings of old tales and contemporary paranormal experiences.

He believes in the mystic power of the arts and that the world we witness is far more mysterious than it appears on the surface.

Subscribe to my newsletter!

Keep connected with me through my website and sign up to my mailing list to keep updated on future releases.

www.adammartinart.uk

Contact Information

Please get in touch with me about anything you would like to ask or share through the channels below, I would love to hear your thoughts.

Email - **adam@adammartinart.uk**
Instagram - **@amartin_art**
Facebook **- Adam Martin Art**

Lightning Source UK Ltd.
Milton Keynes UK
UKHW021333151221
395628UK00006B/95